# INDIE AUTHOR CONFIDENTIAL 12

## SECRETS NO ONE WILL TELL YOU ABOUT BEING A WRITER

M.L. RONN

# CONTENTS


About This Series                                          v
Introduction                                              vii


BECOME A WRITING MASTER

Strategy Change: Become a Writing Master                   3
Studying the Mega Bestsellers More Closely                5
Writing a Journalistic Magazine Article                   9
Lessons in Character Tagging                              11
Craft Lessons from Spyro the Dragon                       15


BECOME A TECHNOLOGY AND
DATA-DRIVEN WRITER

Cold Hard Facts About GPT-3's Editing
Accuracy                                                  19
Accessibility for Authors                                 23
Shutterstock's AI Art Generator                           29
Status Update on AI Proofreading Application              33
Renting a Macintosh in the Cloud                          37


LOOKING FORWARD

The Growing Backlash Against AI Art                        43
The Promise of ChatGPT                                     49
Strategic Defense in the Age of AI                        53
Speaking at Superstars 2023                               55


Content Created While Writing This Book                    65
Read the Next Volume                                       66

Meet M.L. Ronn     67

More Books by M.L. Ronn     69

This isn't your typical writing self-help book. This series is a compilation of lessons learned from an indie author trying to walk the path to success. Follow author M.L. Ronn (Michael La Ronn) as he navigates what it means to master the craft of writing, marketing, and running a profitable publishing business. Learn from his successes and failures, and learn about things that most successful authors only talk about behind the scenes.

To read all the collected volumes of this series in an anthology, visit www.authorlevelup.com/confidential.

# INTRODUCTION

Life happens in cycles. This quarter, I overextended myself and found myself traveling for a lot of events. I was so occupied that I missed my deadline for publishing this volume.

There were times in the past three years where I had so much to write for the *Indie Author Confidential* series that I filled volumes early. In fact, I would write so much that I would have to save content for future volumes. So, I'm not surprised that I find myself on the opposite end of the production spectrum.

What ultimately matters is that I deliver, so here I am. People reading this volume five years from now won't know the difference so long as the volume is published.

## My Core Strategic Priorities

As a refresher, my mission is to create content that entertains and/or educates my audience, preferably both, and to remain nimble in an ever-changing industry. I do this by focusing on three strategic priorities:

- Become a world-class content creator
- Become a technology and data-driven writer
- Become the writer of the future (looking forward)
- Stay tuned for a minor strategy course-correction.

## What's in This Volume

In the Become a World-Class Content Creator section (now renamed to Become a Writing Master), I explain the reason for the name change, new insights I developed from studying mega bestsellers, and lessons in character tagging, to name a few.

In the Become a Technology and Data-Driven Writer section, I discuss my adventures in exploring GPT-3 for editing, accessibility for authors, and renting a Mac in the cloud.

In the Looking Forward section, I discuss the promise of ChatGPT, living strategically in the age of AI, and that oh-so-polarizing topic: AI art.

While the content in this volume is thin, the content most certainly isn't. My journey continues, and every journey has its moments of advancements, moments of rest, and moments of detour.

Enjoy this volume.
--M.L. Ronn
July 3, 2023

# BECOME A WRITING MASTER

# STRATEGY CHANGE: BECOME A WRITING MASTER

With every new year, I take the opportunity to review my strategy. As you know, I have three strategies as an author:

1.  Become a world-class content creator
2.  Become a technology and data-driven writer
3.  Become the writer of the future

I believe my overall strategy is still sound, and it has not changed, but I have decided to change the *name* of one of the strategies.

I've always had a minor issue with "become a world-class content creator." What does world-class mean? Do I want to be world-class, or do I want to be the best?

After thinking about this, I decided I wanted to be a master. I don't want to be good. I don't want to be great. I want to be among the best.

I want to write at the level of mega-bestselling authors. They are more than world-class. This name change clarifies what I really want to achieve.

Therefore, I am officially renaming the first part of my strategy to " Become a Writing Master." This better reflects my goals and gives me higher aspirations to shoot for.

# STUDYING THE MEGA BESTSELLERS MORE CLOSELY

I study the mega bestsellers a lot. I believe they are the best practitioners of the English language, and they're doing many things right because they're selling millions and millions of books.

When I focus on learning the craft, I only want to learn from the masters. No one else matters. That's not to say that mid-list or newer authors don't have anything to teach, but I find that masters are better to study because they execute their techniques more clearly and skillfully on the page. In fact, with many mega bestsellers, you can often see exactly how they pulled off a technique if you know what to look for. Their writing is exceptional, clear, and simple to study.

This quarter, I experimented with a new way of studying the masters. It involves cataloguing techniques and grouping them.

For example, let's say that I encounter a technique by James Patterson that captivates me as a reader. In the past, I would read that scene, break it down, and try to figure out how the author did it. There is nothing wrong with that, and it is effective.

However, this time, as I broke down the scene, I asked myself, "What does this remind me of?"

Maybe Danielle Steel did something similar in one of her novels. If so, how does Patterson's execution of the technique differ from Steel's? How are they similar?

By asking these questions, I can find commonalities and differences. When done enough, the commonalities start to stand out. Perhaps John Grisham, Ken Follett, and James Patterson all do X, but only Nora Roberts does Y. Why did Nora do it, then?

That allows me to build a series of rules I can turn into steps.

Then, I can catalog these techniques based on practicality. When you study every technique you encounter, you don't have much context; when you look for ways to group them, you get more mileage out of your study session. For example, let's take the technique of introducing characters. Maybe I want to know the best way to introduce a main character in a novel. I would start by looking at main characters that resonated with me from mega-bestseller books I enjoyed.

But a main character differs from a supporting character, and a supporting character differs from a minor character. Therefore, I could neatly chunk character techniques into groups. When taken further, I can track other elements of characterization, such as character tags, the execution of back story, and more. With careful note-taking and a bit of foresight, I have notes that are immediately practical. If I'm writing a short story and I'm practicing minor characters, I can pull out my notes, look at the steps, and get instant feedback on how the mega bestsellers are doing it. That's powerful.

Anyway, studying the craft is not something anyone can teach you. It's very much a figure-it-out-yourself game. Despite the thousands of writing books out there, every writer must find their own path. This is mine.

# WRITING A JOURNALISTIC MAGAZINE ARTICLE

I wrote an article for *Indie Author Magazine* (IAM). *IAM* is a new magazine aimed at helping others learn the advice and tools they need to succeed in today's digital world. The magazine takes a journalistic, fact-based approach to its articles. It also specializes in tools and holds an annual conference called the Author Tech Summit, where they invite speakers who demonstrate tools and walk authors through them to help them understand what is available.

I pitched the magazine with a few article ideas and had a quick call with the editor-in-chief. I like the magazine, its mission, and the management team's vision for where they want it to go. I believe there is value in taking a journalistic approach, as it will become a differentiating factor that helps the magazine stand out and be known for its objective voice. It's a refreshing approach to writing advice.

My first article for the magazine was titled "Managing Your Author Career with Chronic Illness: A Health Coach's Perspective." I interviewed my friend and author Roland Denzel, a fitness and nutrition coach who helps people live their healthiest lives. He has written books and given interviews with health tips, making him the first person I thought of for this topic.

I interviewed Roland on a Zoom call for about 15 minutes, asking him for his perspective on managing chronic illness. I recorded the call and used his quotes in the article.

After the article went through the editorial process, I received the final production copy of the magazine. Roland was pleased with the article and that I didn't take anything he said out of context. To me, this was a sign that I did a good job.

Writing this article was different from my usual writing, as much of what I write is based on my opinion. It was a good exercise to stretch my skills and write something different for a change.

# LESSONS IN CHARACTER TAGGING

I recently reread *The Rithmatist* by Brandon Sanderson and found some great elements in the book to study. Brandon Sanderson is one of the most successful fantasy authors alive. He has sold millions of books, and he has adopted and championed many of the new ways of marketing that the ever-changing digital world offers. Anyone as successful as him is doing a few things right!

*The Rithmatist* is a young adult novel. It's a bildungsroman, to be specific. Not only is it a great novel, but it is also quite easy to study.

One thing that Sanderson did in the novel that was clear and transparent (to me) was how he addressed character tagging. Character tagging is a personality trait or action repeated throughout the text to 1) help readers distinguish between characters and 2) help the author make characters more memorable. Character tags are used in every medium, and it is perhaps the easiest to see them at work in television and in movies. Think about your favorite movie character. What is the first thing you remember about them? Chances are, it's probably a tag. Clark Kent wears a suit and glasses. He is meek and anxious. But

Superman wears a blue costume with a flowing red cape. He does not wear glasses, and he is confident and unflappable. These traits illustrate the difference between the two characters.

The Teenage Mutant Ninja Turtles also have classic character tags. Each turtle uses a unique weapon. Each turtle has a unique color. Each turtle also has a unique personality; Leonardo is serious and bossy, Raphael is a hothead, Donatello is a brainiac, and Michelangelo is a party dude.

Carmen Sandiego is a master thief who pulls off incredible capers. Even if you have never consumed Carmen Sandiego stories, you probably recognize her trademark red trench coat and fedora.

That's how character tags work. They make characters more memorable. In a full cast of characters, they help distinguish between the characters. They are an incredibly useful tool, though I didn't understand their true power until relatively recently when I took a course from Dean Wesley Smith. His course helped me "see" tags everywhere. They are so ubiquitous that they are almost invisible. Fortunately, though, once you understand them, they are amazingly simple to use.

In this chapter, I will distill my main observations about tags and how I use them intentionally in my work.

Now that I've described what tags are and why they are important, let's cover some basics. When should you use them?

Ideally, the most important time to introduce a character tag is when you introduce a character. It sounds obvious, but there are some pitfalls. First, for something to be a tag, it has to be used more than once. If you only introduce a character trait once, readers will probably forget. Or, you could introduce a really cool tag, only never to use it again. The key is to pick one or two tags and make those the only ones. Then, repeat the tag at least the first three times the reader meets the character. There is such a thing as going overboard with a tag, so you don't have to use it every single time, but you have to use it enough to keep it top of mind and hammer into the reader's head that the tag exists. Once you've done that, you don't have to do it as often. You only need to do it the first three times, then maybe every other time after that.

I like to think about tag repetition like building a relationship. When you first meet someone, you get a first impression. When you meet them a second time, you get the same impression, but you see another side of that person. Every encounter builds a multifaceted, multidimensional understanding of that person. Characters are the same way. This is why the best tagging is intentional.

The reason I like *The Rithmatist* so much as an illustrative lesson in tagging is because tagging is so simple. Every character only has one major tag.

As I mentioned, this novel is a young adult novel. Generally, I try to only study adult novels because the craft differences are quite vast between the two genres when you study them. However, young adult novels are perfect for studying tags because the authors make them simpler. You can see them at work more easily than in thrillers or science fiction, where authors follow the same basic techniques but do more advanced executions. In young adult novels, everything has to be clear and simple so that young adults can grasp and enjoy it. I'm not saying that young adult novels are simple or dumbed down. I'm simply saying that the language is usually simpler. Simple does not mean easy, and young adult novels are just as challenging to write as adult novels. The execution is different, that's all. This makes them great examples to study, but only if you study novels from professional, prolific authors like Brandon Sanderson. Sanderson is another great author to study because he writes both adult and young fiction, so he understands both worlds. This makes him a great author to learn from.

In any case, the following list constitutes my current approach to character tags based on my learnings from Sanderson:

1. Determine at least one character trait and one physical trait I want to tag when introducing the character.
2. Upon introducing that character, introduce the tag.
3. Avoid false tags, i.e., tags that I may never use again. Keep only the tags that I intend to use.
4. Repeat the tags the second and third times the reader meets the character to "hammer" it in that these traits are important.
5. Repeat the tags regularly throughout the novel without overdoing them.
6. If a series, repeat the tags, *especially* when readers meet the character in subsequent books in the series.
7. Use many tags for main characters; they don't all need to be introduced at once. There are physical tags, personality tags, history tags, expression tags, and so much more, especially with first-person POV characters.
8. The more time I spend on a tag, the more important it is.

That's just a high level. Tagging is more complicated and nuanced than this, but these guidelines have helped me make my characters clearer and more memorable.

# CRAFT LESSONS FROM SPYRO THE DRAGON

I bought my daughter a Nintendo Switch, and, because I couldn't help myself, I also bought myself a few video games. One of them was the *Spyro: Reignited Trilogy,* a modern remake of the original Spyro the Dragon trilogy for PlayStation.

I loved the Spyro games when I was a kid and played them for hours. The series follows a young dragon and his firefly companion on various quests to save the world. In the first game, Spyro must rescue his elder dragons, who have been turned into crystal statues. In the second game, he jumps into a portal to go on vacation, only to end up in a completely different world where a supervillain sorcerer threatens to take over. In the third game, he must rescue the dragon eggs of his kingdom from an evil sorceress.

The games are classic platformers that require the player to defeat enemies, collect gems, and complete various mini-game challenges. They are great fun, and the remake did not disappoint. It made me feel like a kid again and reminded me of a lesson in writing craft that I have learned over the years, but continue to learn in different ways: teams.

The first Spyro game was an instant classic. It had amazing

gameplay for its time, unique exploration of diverse worlds, and an unbelievable soundtrack by Stewart Copeland, the drummer for The Police. Honestly, the soundtrack was the best part of the first game.

What the first game didn't have was an engaging story. In the opening movie, one of Spyro's elder dragons gives a media interview in which he insults a recurring series villain named Gnasty Gnorc. Gnasty sees the interview and goes ballistic, casting a spell that turns all of the elder dragons into crystal statues, but somehow misses Spyro. Then Spyro sets off on his quest. The story was quite lacking, and the ending was anticlimactic.

*Spyro 2: Ripto's Rage* is a much different game. In this game, Spyro and his firefly companion, Sparx, are heading to the beach for vacation. The portal they travel through doesn't take them to the beach, though—it delivers them to another world called Glimmer. Upon arriving, Spyro discovers that a team of characters summoned him to the world to stop a madman sorcerer named Ripto who is trying to take over the new world. Spyro must work with this newfound team to stop Ripto.

The team consists of a faun named Elora, who serves as a love interest of sorts; a cheetah named Hunter who is handy with a bow and technology; a fairy named Zoe who gives Spyro advice; and last but not least, a greedy banker named Moneybags who sells Spyro new skills as he collects gems across the world. Spyro's team is endearing and memorable, and they appear again in the third game in the series.

The stories between *Spyro 1* and *Spyro 2* couldn't be more different. The second game does a much better job of telling an engaging story. All these years later, I still remember the team fondly. That's the key. Readers remember teams. You can never go wrong with a team in your story.

That's the lesson Spyro helped me relearn yet again.

# BECOME A TECHNOLOGY AND DATA-DRIVEN WRITER

# COLD HARD FACTS ABOUT GPT-3'S EDITING ACCURACY

When I test something, I test everything about it. Now that I know that GPT-3 is a viable proofreading solution, I wanted to put some numbers to it. Sure, it's good, but just how good? How does it compare to Microsoft Word's Editor, Grammarly's free version, Grammarly's premium version, and ProWritingAid? I performed an in-depth test to help me determine the cold hard facts.

For this test, I dictated approximately 1,500 words of text toward a work in progress. I copied that text into several identical Microsoft Word files and enabled track changes. In each file, I tested one of the grammar-checking apps: Microsoft Word's Editor, Grammarly's free version, Grammarly's premium version, ProWritingAid, and GPT-3. I went through each checker's suggestions, only correcting the issues that I agreed with. Once done, I ran a quick macro to count the number of track changes in each document.

Next, I created an Excel spreadsheet that listed each edit and tracked which grammar checker caught it. For example, GPT-3 might catch an error that Grammarly's premium version missed, and vice versa.

Building the spreadsheet was a painstaking task because I had to compare the track changes in each document to verify which checkers caught it, but it was worth it. When I was done, I had a comprehensive report with conclusions that surprised even me.

There were a total of 89 edits. Microsoft Word's Editor caught 3, ProWritingAid caught 8, Grammarly's free version caught 12, Grammarly's premium version caught 33, and GPT-3 also caught 33.

Between Grammarly's premium version and GPT-3, the two checkers caught 20 items in common.

Microsoft Word and ProWritingAid were the biggest losers in this test; neither of them caught any errors that Grammarly's free version or GPT-3 didn't catch. Therefore, I could have turned off both of these checkers and it wouldn't have made a difference.

Grammarly's premium version excelled in two key areas: punctuation and conciseness. GPT-3 won big in advanced grammar rules, missing words and articles, and formatting errors. Both checkers were a tossup in almost every other category. In some, Grammarly's premium version caught one or two more than GPT-3; in others, it was the other way around.

I find it fascinating that GPT-3 and Grammarly's premium version caught the same number of errors. I also find it fascinating that the errors they caught were mostly the same, but the ones they specialized in were extremely unique.

I also found that Grammarly's premium version is definitely worth the value, despite (in my opinion) producing a lot of noise. I don't dislike Grammarly's premium version, but my biggest frustration with the app is that you can't control which suggestions it recommends. You have to read through all of them, many of which do not apply to professional writers or are downright wrong. I wish I could customize Grammarly's premium version so that it only provides the checks I care about, much like I can with ProWritingAid. But it is what it is.

Anyway, this taught me that I need to revise my workflow. As much as I like using Microsoft Word and ProWritingAid, it appears I no longer need them for my editing workflow, at least not until they improve.

The data also led me to the following workflow:

1. I upload my dictation audio files to my computer, where Dragon auto-transcribes the audio files.
2. I open the files in Microsoft Word, run my dictation macro to clean up the text, then close the file.
3. I run my new GPT-3 editing app that passes the file through GPT-3 and builds a track changes comparison document that I can review.
4. I review GPT-3's changes and accept the ones I want.
5. I run Grammarly's premium version on the remaining errors. This dramatically cuts down the number of suggestions that Grammarly makes because GPT-3 will have already fixed most of them. Therefore, the "suggestion noise" that Grammarly is infamous for is significantly reduced, allowing me to spend less time reviewing these edits.

As a final step of this process, I self-edit the text like I would normally, finding the remaining errors and restructuring the text as I see fit.

As I mentioned in a previous chapter, I engineered my GPT-3 tool to automatically be compatible with GPT-4. Who knows how much more powerful GPT-4 will be? It might not be any more powerful, but it could also bring it closer to eliminating the need for Grammarly. I don't think that will ever happen, though. Grammarly does some things really well, and within a few years, I expect they will launch a counter move, improving the accuracy of their spell-checker. I expect ProWritingAid will also follow suit with updates to its software, possibly even integrating GPT into its product. This is just pure speculation on my part, but I have a hard time believing that existing grammar checkers will roll over as OpenAI attempts to destroy their market share. This level of competition is wonderful because when these companies compete, we reap the benefits. In my case, as they improve, I cannot lose because I have all of them!

It just shows you that no process in any writer's business is sacrosanct; one should not be afraid to revisit their processes to ensure they are still efficient. You never know where the data will lead.

# ACCESSIBILITY FOR AUTHORS

While visiting Saudi Arabia, I met an American and a Canadian who specialize in accessibility for authors and publishers. They were guest speakers at the conference I attended, as the Saudi Ministry of Literature and Education has prioritized making Arabic books accessible to its blind population. The two experts I met, Michael Johnson and Laura Brady, are two of the world's preeminent experts in accessibility for books. It was a pleasure to meet them and spend time with them.

While strolling along the picturesque corniches along the Red Sea, we discussed accessibility and its challenges.

The simplest definition of accessibility is this: making every book accessible so that anyone in the world can read it. Sighted people can pick up a book and read it; they can also download an e-book into their preferred device and read that way as well. However, low-sighted and blind individuals cannot do this.

Making books accessible for the blind is incredibly important because it allows visually impaired individuals to have the same access to knowledge and information as those who can see.

This is not only a matter of fairness and equality, but it also helps to promote inclusivity and diversity in the literary world.

Audiobooks are also another accessibility avenue. Audiobooks are recordings of books being read aloud and can be listened to on devices such as smartphones or computers, narrated by either a human or an AI. This makes it possible for the blind to listen to books and enjoy the same level of access to literature as sighted individuals.

There is, of course, also braille. Braille is a system of raised dots that can be felt with the fingers and used to read text. Books can be printed in braille, or they can be converted into braille using a braille embosser. Braille books are typically much heavier and bulkier than regular books, but they provide the same level of access to literature for the blind.

Another way to make books accessible is through the use of large print editions. These books have larger fonts and text modifications to make them easier for readers with poor eyesight to read more easily. Many self-published authors have begun creating large print editions, but not all books in this format are profitable ventures.

Additionally, many e-book readers now include built-in accessibility features such as text-to-speech and support for braille displays. This means blind individuals can use these devices to read e-books as sighted individuals do. This is a great option for those who prefer to read e-books, as it allows them to enjoy the convenience of digital reading.

Making books accessible for the blind is not only the right thing to do, but it also makes good business sense. By making books accessible to a wider audience, authors can increase their potential readership and reach new audiences.

There's also the issue of compliance. In Europe, for example, publishers will soon be required to make their books accessible or face heavy fines. So, accessibility is a compliance and legal issue too.

I cannot emphasize enough that the advent of e-books has been a tremendous gift to blind readers because they can use text-to-voice features built into devices such as the Kindle, smartphones, and Kobo e-readers. They can read on any device. Because of this, many low-vision and blind readers prefer e-books as their primary reading method.

Despite this advancement in making books more accessible, some challenges remain. First, just because a book exists in e-book format doesn't mean it plays nicely with a reading app when an underserved individual is using it. E-books are HTML files, and it takes some special programming work for under-served individuals to read them as the author intended. Second, most authors and publishers don't know about these communi-ties' reading preferences, and even if they did, they don't always have the skills to tweak their HTML to make it accessible. Third, it can be expensive and time-consuming to hire help to make an entire catalog of books accessible.

For these reasons, accessibility is rarely discussed in the author and publisher community. Traditional publishers understand this issue more than most, and they take steps in the right direction, but they are burdened by bureaucracy and cumbersome workflows that prevent them from solving this problem easily. Most self-published authors don't even think about accessibility, but it is perhaps easier for them to meet its challenges than traditional publishers.

So, what is an author to do? Over lunch, I asked Michael and Laura about the top three most common challenges and how to fix them. They told me and also gave me links to tools I could download for free to check just how accessible my books were. These tools would also diagnose any problems so that I could research how to fix them.

Later that night, in my hotel room, I downloaded these tools and tested one of my books. Unfortunately, I failed the accessibility test on a few critical points. In researching the errors, I discovered they weren't difficult to fix. In fact, with just a few quick Google searches and setting tweaks in Vellum (my preferred formatting app), I got my book to pass both EPUB Check and Ace+ accessibility checks by Daisy, two critical tests that gauge how accessible a book may be. While these tests are not 100 percent determinative, they're a good start.

I sketched out a new workflow to ensure future accessibility for my books, outlining potential pitfalls I needed to account for, such as images. Thirty minutes later, I had a winning plan and accessible books!

Were they perfectly accessible? Absolutely not. There is a reason why professional formatters are hired to make books accessible. Nothing any current writing app can do will be better than a good, hand-coded e-book by a professional. However, because most authors are probably using a dedicated formatting app, they will not want to also hire a formatter. Doing so is a maintenance headache because you have to pay the formatter to make basic changes.

But for those authors who use Vellum, accessibility is quite easy. Make sure that Vellum generates EPUB 3.0, that your images have alt tags, and that your table of contents makes sense. Assuming you have a relatively straightforward book, and assuming you can make these changes, you can probably do exactly what I did.

In thinking about this further, it made me upset that traditional publishers can't do the same thing. In less than a month, I got my 80 books to pass accessibility checks. You're telling me that multibillion-dollar companies can also do the same thing?

In my opinion, there's no reason this problem should exist.

This is something we should have settled back in 2004 or 2005 with the advent of the e-book. But alas, here we are.

I believe indie authors can play a role in the accessibility space and win. Think about it: traditional publishers are not serving this community. They want to, and they mean well, but they don't seem capable of it. In just a few clicks, we can. Think about people in the blind and low-sight community who could discover our books, read them, and become fans! It's a win for them and it's a win for us.

Michael Johnson challenged me to write a book about disability for authors to promote this goal. I took him up on that, and I plan on writing this book in the future. Some things I will need to explore before I write it include:

- Speaking with blind and low-sight individuals to better understand their preferences and the day-to-day mechanics of how they read.
- Finding quick wins for others who do not use Vellum. What about authors who use a writing app that doesn't produce accessible EPUBs? What steps would those authors need to take? This effort will fail if it is not easy. Whatever solutions I find need to be so easy that authors can implement them in less than one hour. They must also integrate into many workflows. Otherwise, it won't be convenient.
- Learning how to write about this topic in the most basic terms.

I don't think this book needs to be long. I can probably say everything I need to say in 5,000 words or less (but don't hold me to that!). The most important thing is using my platform to get the message out there that creating accessible e-books is easy, cost-effective, not time-consuming, not technical, and most importantly--the right thing to do. If I can do that while also creating an evergreen book, I hope I can do some good in the world.

In any case, I expect to be talking about accessibility more frequently in the near future.

# SHUTTERSTOCK'S AI ART GENERATOR

Never in my life have I seen a technology move as fast as artificial intelligence art. I am astounded by how rapidly the technology is evolving. There have been so many advancements that it makes my head spin.

In late January 2023, Shutterstock, one of the largest stock media companies in the world, unveiled its new AI art generator, created in conjunction with LG AI and OpenAI's DALL-e. This partnership has been in the works for a while, but it is just now bearing fruit. Shutterstock has been quite involved in AI investments and research for the last few years. I recall watching one of their executives give a presentation about how interested they were in the technology at an online digital conference. So, it was not a surprise to see them roll out their own AI art generator. What was a surprise, however, was how they executed it.

Shutterstock sits on one of the largest repositories of stock photos in the world. It goes without saying that they of course have the rights to use their database to train an AI model.

What happens when you have a dataset that is safe to use? Well, you have an AI art generator that you can use with reasonable confidence that you won't infringe upon the copyrights or trademarks of another person. At least, not knowingly.

Shutterstock's terms of service dictate that you can use the AI art generator with the same licenses that the company already offers on its website, with the same great benefits and liability guarantees that the company offers. This is huge, and I cannot understate how critical it is for creators. The only caveat is that you must not use the AI-generated image to infringe on anyone's intellectual property. You also cannot use the AI image for nefarious reasons. I believe this caveat exists only to prevent idiots who don't know any better from creating images of Spider-Man, Mickey Mouse, and other trademarked characters. It also disincentivizes people from using living artists in their prompts. From what I can tell, as long as you don't use copyrighted or trademarked material in your prompts, and you scrutinize your images carefully for trademarks, it will be pretty difficult for you to get sued because 1) Shutterstock has presumably cleared the copyrights for the images in the dataset, 2) generating an AI image is contemplated within that license, 3) you are not knowingly infringing on anyone's copyright, and 4) you will have done as much due diligence as one can.

Also, to Shutterstock's credit, they are compensating the creators of images in the dataset. If a creator's image is used in a downloaded image, they receive a payment. We can debate how much they receive and whether it's enough, but at least Shutterstock took this critical step. For this reason, I predict that most artists will look the other way and focus their ire on companies that do not offer any compensation at all.

The second problem is that we still haven't settled the fair use issue. Can a company train an AI model with copyrighted data? If they don't have permission for the images in the training, does it constitute fair use? If the company does have permission and the terms of service the creator signs include AI art generation, does that settle it?

When a user generates an AI image based on various copyrighted images, does it constitute fair use, is it a derivative work, or is it a new work altogether?

Based on the conversations I've seen with lawyers, artists, technologists, and other interested professionals, I believe that training an AI model with copyrighted data constitutes fair use, even if it's profit-oriented. However, using AI art generators with copyrighted data without the creators' permission *could* constitute copyright infringement. Therefore, before I use such an AI art generator, I would need more assurances from Shutterstock than I am currently getting. I would need to know without a shadow of a doubt that all the images in their database are cleared. Furthermore, I would also need to know the terms of service that content creators sign when uploading their photos to the site. Finally, I would need to know the company is taking necessary steps to prevent scammers from uploading AI-generated images to the site and having those included in the AI model.

While researching this topic, I found at least a dozen YouTube videos of scammers teaching people how to upload images from MidJourney and Stable Diffusion onto Shutterstock, even though the website bans these images. This is a serious problem, and even though Shutterstock *says* they have all copyrights cleared, that may not be the case if images uploaded after July 2022 are included in the model's training.

That said, Shutterstock deserves credit because they appear to be doing this correctly. However, their AI art generator isn't very good right now. It doesn't generate people well. It reminds me of early versions of MidJourney. But knowing what I know about MidJourney, they updated their models rapidly. I expect within a year or two, Shutterstock's models will be on par with current AI art generators. When that happens, the game will change. Imagine needing to find a specific image on Shutterstock and not finding it. All you have to do is click their AI art generator, generate the image you need and purchase it. That's the future, and it's here now.

Anyone who laments this doesn't understand the problems heavy stock image users face. There simply aren't enough artists to create all the images people need. I can't tell you how many times I have searched for an image on stock photo sites to no avail.

Now that we have a viable solution to meet virtually any image need, I predict many stock photo companies will follow Shutterstock, but many will also go out of business for failing to adapt.

# STATUS UPDATE ON AI PROOFREADING APPLICATION

In an earlier chapter, I mentioned that I wanted to create an application using GPT-3 to edit my work. This is because the language model is a fantastic proofreader. The purpose of this chapter is to document my findings from working with two developers on this application.

The thing about artificial intelligence is that it is uncharted territory for writers. Therefore, when I went into this project, I didn't have any real certainty if it would work. Either it would be amazingly successful or it would spontaneously combust. The only way to know was to dive in.

In researching this technology extensively, I discovered three ways to approach this application.

The first way is to hope that a writing app developer integrates the OpenAI API into existing writing apps. Imagine writing your novel, clicking a button, and watching edits appear as tracked changes before your eyes. All you would have to do is supply your OpenAI API key, in which case you would be responsible for the cost of calling the API.

As a side note, I'd also like to point out that Microsoft Word is another viable (if not the best) positioned app to address this problem. After all, OpenAI is mostly owned by Microsoft, and the company has announced plans to bring the ChatGPT API to its applications. Whether or not they will allow you to use the language models for editing remains to be seen.

The second path involves Google Docs. Google Docs supports Google Apps Scripts, Google's high-powered version of macros. Google Apps Scripts can do much more than Visual Basic for Applications (VBA) and can also call APIs. I hired a developer specializing in this programming language and asked him to develop an application that could call the OpenAI API and return edited text as tracked changes. It turns out it could be done, but there were some limitations. First, the developer ran into an issue where the script called the API too many times, resulting in excessive API costs. The script also did not do well with text longer than 500 words. Unfortunately, we could not find a successful way around these problems. It's unfortunate because I thought Google Docs would be a great and easy way for everyday users to experience and utilize the power of GPT-3. After all, just about everyone can watch a quick YouTube installation video and click a few buttons to run a script. Also, everyone knows how to copy and paste text into a Google Doc. To me, this was the path of least resistance and worth exploring just in case it could help someone. But, alas.

The third way of solving this problem was through Microsoft Word and Python. Word and Python work well together, and you can write code to accomplish many tasks between them.

Python is also more flexible because it is a universal programming language. A good developer can do almost anything with it.

I hired another developer to build a prototype application. Here's how it works:

- I upload a Word document to the application.
- The application breaks the Word document into approximately 500-word chunks. Each chunk represents one call to the API.
- Before passing the text through the API, the application tokenizes the text.
- The application passes the text through the API one chunk at a time.
- The OpenAI API edits the text, then passes the chunks back to the application.
- The application takes the chunks and rebuilds them in a new Word document, recreating any formatting that existed in the original document, including fonts, font sizes, indentation, and formatting styles such as headers, bullets, bolds, italics, and underlines.
- The application uses Microsoft Word's Compare feature to build a comparison document that shows the track changes between the original and the revised.

And that's it. I have the power of GPT-3, GPT-4, and ChatGPT at my fingertips to use whenever I want. And it's cheap. At the time of this writing, I pay two cents per 1,000 tokens (about 750 words). A 500-word chunk technically is counted twice because OpenAI has to read the text and then generate it again, so 500 words are actually 1,000 words. So, a 500-word writing session is two cents. I shake my head every time I think about the cost. Even crazier, the costs are decreasing. It used to be six cents per 1,000 tokens!

The Python application is also useful because it is future-ready. For example, I am now limited to GPT-3, which is not a good editor. However, the ChatGPT API will soon be available, and I will be able to hook into that—all I have to do is update the API model. We built that flexibility so I can immediately take advantage of new models and improvements to existing models without rehiring the developer. I am positive I will have to rehire him at some point, but we are doing our best to avoid that.

Using GPT models to assist in editing will be the future, and I'm glad to be experimenting with these models as an early adopter.

# RENTING A MACINTOSH IN THE CLOUD

I've written numerous times in this series about my experiences while writing and traveling. Sometimes, I've been highly successful and productive, but other times, my productivity has suffered. It depends on the type of trip, my energy levels, and the time I have available.

This year, I have a lot of travel planned: family gatherings, work trips, and writing conferences. It will be my busiest travel year since 2019, and that's saying a lot, because I traveled a lot in 2022.

This quarter, I'm attending the Superstars Writing Seminar in Colorado Springs, Colorado.

I'm used to bringing copies of my PowerPoint presentations to events—it's the definition of being prepared. However, I'm not used to bringing my own computer. I prefer not to do that.

However, this event presents a different problem: I'll be there for a week. Usually, I'm only at events for two or three days. This time, I'll be away for six days. Because of this, I need a workstation to continue my writing.

I have a high-powered MacBook Pro, and I don't like to take

it away from home. It is my main computer, and I take great care to protect it.

I have a spare Mac computer, which I used before purchasing my MacBook Pro. It's an older Mac with limited RAM and hard drive space, but it's sufficient for checking my emails and browsing the Internet. It can't run most applications, including Microsoft Word and Dragon, but I would like to be able to dictate, transcribe, and edit my text while at the conference. I don't want to purchase a new computer.

I sound like I'm complaining, but I promise I'm not. I saw this as an interesting challenge to find a tool to help me with this problem. Fortunately, after doing some research, I encountered a service called "Mac in Cloud," which is a Mac virtualization service that allows you to rent a Mac computer that operates in the cloud. It is primarily a tool for developers to test Mac versions of their applications when they don't have physical Mac computers. The service offers a pay-as-you-go plan that allows you to rent a late-model Mac operating system for one dollar an hour. It comes with dozens of applications pre-installed, including Microsoft Office, Vellum, and many more. The only downside is that while you can install applications from the Mac App Store, you cannot install anything outside of the store. Custom applications are not allowed. This means that I cannot install off-the-beaten-path applications that don't exist in the Mac App Store. I also cannot install the custom Whisper application that I developed late last year. Again, somewhat unfortunate, but not the end of the world.

I can't install Microsoft Word on my older Mac because there isn't enough space. I also can't install Vellum. However, I can run both of these programs in the cloud using my old Mac. And it only costs me one dollar per hour. Mac in Cloud worked really well for me while I was on the road.

It just goes to show you that there are tools to help you solve virtually every problem. You just have to be willing to search for them and find unusual ways to chain them together. It's an exciting time to be alive, especially now that we are in the advent of what appears to be AI wars between Google and Microsoft.

Also, using the Mac in Cloud service gave me a great idea for a YouTube video teaching Windows users how to use Vellum on their Windows machine easily and with no strings attached—just one dollar per hour. That's an easy pill to swallow if you ask me.

# LOOKING FORWARD

# THE GROWING BACKLASH AGAINST AI ART

There are several third rails in the publishing industry that, if touched, will galvanize hundreds if not thousands of people to line up on digital forms and try to cancel you.

One of those rails is the topic of literary agents. Another is developmental editing. The third (and newest) rail is artificial intelligence art.

I wrote extensively in the last two volumes of this series about my thoughts on artificial intelligence art and how writers of the future will be able to apply it to further their careers. You should know how I feel about the technology at this point.

However, AI art is so polarizing that you can't even *mention* it without pissing people off.

Case in point: I mentioned the applications of this technology in one of my nightly blog posts. A subscriber replied and told me how disappointed they were that I would even think to promote this technology because it is theft.

And that was just for *mentioning* AI art!

I received further backlash by demoing MidJourney with my friend Matty Dalrymple on her show "The Indy Author Podcast." I spent an hour walking through the tool, explaining its use, and demonstrating simple use cases. Again, some folks didn't like that, and I got the moral lecture about how I was taking jobs away from artists and how I should be ashamed of myself.

All of this is unfortunate. Again, it shows just how short-sighted people are.

I will be the first person to tell you that I support artists. But we can't even discuss AI art. People on both sides draw the lines so that you're either for artists or against artists, and that is the problem. While I believe some problems with AI art and copyright need to be resolved, the genie is out of the bottle. As much as you like or don't like AI art, it doesn't matter. It's not going away, just like Facebook and other social media networks will continue to use your data for nefarious purposes regardless of whether you cancel your account. If you choose not to use something based on principle, that's fine—no one is forcing you to use the tool. But if I know anything about history, I will bet good money in Vegas that many of the current detractors of AI art will be using it within a decade. They will conveniently forget their current vitriol against the technology.

I wish more people would see this debate for what it is: mostly smoke and mirrors. At the heart of the issue is a topic that virtually all *professionals* in the author community agrees on: AI art companies should *not* be using the work of living artists whose work is protected by copyright without licensing it or obtaining their permission. We all share a common goal, and we should do what we can to support those fighting for it. This means signing petitions, sending emails to these companies, and, for those who have means, filing lawsuits to force the courts to hopefully rule in our favor.

However, we shouldn't confuse the central issue. Yes, copyright infringement and lack of payment to artists are unequivocally bad, but that doesn't mean the tool itself is bad. It also doesn't mean that AI art should be completely banned. Some in the artist community would prefer that the technology never be used, ever, and that's a colossal mistake.

I also think people are confused about the true impact of the technology. I've seen people argue that it will take away work from artists. I won't deny that, but we should clarify exactly who will be losing work.

Artists with corporate clientele are the ones who stand the most to lose from AI art. Traditional publishers commonly hire illustrators for their book covers, particularly in the fantasy genre. These artists face threats on two fronts:

1. Traditional publishers won't need to hire them anymore because they have a tool that can replace them.
2. Authors will copy their style now that they have a tool that can imitate them. Some of these imitations will be similar in style; others will be blatant copyright infringement. But in either case, the damage is done.

We should be concerned about corporate clients abandoning artists because that's what they will do, especially when they're looking to cut costs. Many companies will do what they can legally get away with.

But we need to be honest about something: these artists likely wouldn't have worked with 99 percent of the authors copying them anyway. So, I don't believe that *authors* are taking away much work from artists. Generally, the more expensive something is, the less likely and/or willing authors are to pay for it. Artists are expensive, especially when authors want to create art for things that don't generate profits, such as character illustrations or bookmarks.

Now, do I believe that authors should use AI art to copy the style of living artists? No. I do not use living artists or copyrighted work in my AI art prompts out of respect for artists. But to boycott the technology altogether would be unwise.

Also, the costs of design continue to increase. In less than a decade, authors may have no choice but to use AI art since many cover designers and illustrators will become unaffordable for all but the most affluent authors.

Even if you try to avoid AI art, you may not be able to. How will you know for sure if a designer isn't using AI art in their designs on your book cover? How will you know for sure if a stock photo you buy wasn't generated at least partially by an AI? It's not exactly easy to determine if an image was AI-generated, and there aren't tools sophisticated enough to do this yet.

This is a difficult, thorny issue with no clear-cut answers. No matter what happens, artists will win, and they will lose. I pity the court that has to settle AI art copyright issues.

There are so many questions that the law will have to contend with:

- Can a company scrape the Internet and use copyrighted content to train its models without compensating the artists of that material?
- Who owns the copyright to AI art?
- If AI art companies are to compensate artists, what does that look like? Who pays for it? The company, the consumer, or both?
- Who determines how much an artist gets paid? What if the artist and the AI art company don't agree?
- Can artists "opt out" of AI art models, or has that ship already sailed?

- Can cryptocurrency solve some of the logistical issues with compensating artists? Is this a good use case for blockchain and microtransactions?
- Will AI programs be valuable if they cannot use copyrighted material in their models?

There are so many more questions. Regardless of how these first lawsuits pan out, I know one thing for sure: we will be even more confused about the application of AI art and the answers to the questions I posed before the lawsuits began. We are potentially looking at a hellscape where no one can use this technology with any real certainty.

Lawsuits alone aren't going to settle this. Legislators will also have to get involved. Considering that we do not have a functioning Congress in the United States, we may have to live with uncertainty for a long time.

In the meantime, I wish the conversation would center on facts instead of emotions and virtue signaling. We should make no mistake: however these issues get resolved for artists, that is almost precisely how they will be resolved for authors when AI becomes sophisticated enough to write full-length novels and short stories.

Here is a strategy I think smart authors should follow.

First, begin experimenting with the technology and learn how to master it.

Second, don't deploy the technology just yet. Keep an eye on the courts and legislatures that will hopefully settle some of the low-hanging fruit in the next few years.

Next, as some of these issues get resolved, look for opportunities. For me, the opportunities are areas where you can deploy AI art safely and productively without worrying about legal quagmires. These opportunities should also help you minimize expenses and grow your income. The opportunities may be narrow at first; that's typically how things go. However, if you remain on the lookout for them, you'll gain first and early-mover advantages.

Finally, operate under the assumption that this technology will not be stopped. It will change your decisions and help you prepare for the moment when these issues get settled, potentially in our favor. Don't be the author who misses out on an opportunity because you weren't paying attention.

# THE PROMISE OF CHATGPT

In November 2022, OpenAI released a research preview of their new tool ChatGPT.

ChatGPT is a computer program that can understand and produce human-like language. It is trained on a large dataset of text from the internet and can do various tasks such as generate text, answer questions, complete prompts, and engage in conversation. It can be used for things like writing essays, creating chatbots, and even generating creative content like stories. It is a powerful tool for many industries and applications.

Believe it or not, the last paragraph was written by the software! It truly is incredible. I like to think of it as the fourth dimension of search engines. Many people use ChatGPT to answer common questions such as:

- Who is X?
- Give me some gift ideas for Valentine's Day, or
- Write an article about the London Book Fair.

The software has a few limitations. First, the current research preview is trained only through 2021. You can't ask it anything about current events, and it is known to give bad and or misleading advice. You would have to be stupid to use it in any of these capacities. Also, you can only use it in a browser, and the demand is so high that you sometimes have to wait in a queue. Also, ChatGPT cannot infer between prompts. If you ask it a question, it cannot remember what you asked it previously. I trust that all of these things will change in due time.

Anyway, I was watching a YouTube video from a fellow author and YouTuber, and I discovered that ChatGPT could also edit text.

In a previous volume of the series, I wrote about OpenAI's Whisper speech recognition model, which can be used for dictation. I also wrote about how the OpenAI team managed to solve some roadblocks that have held back the field of natural language processing for a while: issues related to part of speech tagging. For example, there's a reason why tools like Grammarly and ProWritingAid still can't recognize the difference between the words "to" and "too." This is because, to do this, they have to understand the parts of speech of the sentence and the relationship between them. This is incredibly difficult in English.

Somehow, Whisper solves this problem. Therefore, I wasn't surprised to see that ChatGPT can perform more sophisticated spelling and grammar checks than current tools on the market. For example, if I tell ChatGPT to fix a section of text for typos only, it will hunt for typos and leave the rest of the text alone.

This is remarkable. I ran some tests using a recent manuscript that my editor reviewed. I pulled out the sentences that my editor flagged with typos, spelling, and grammatical errors. Examples include lay versus lie, missing articles, and more. I ran the original sentences through Microsoft Word's Editor, Grammarly, ProWritingAid, and PerfectIt. Naturally, because I ran these tools on the text before sending them to my editor, they didn't catch the issues she flagged.

However, when I ran this same text through ChatGPT, it found approximately 60 percent of the issues that my editor flagged. The results were outstanding. This led me to the following conclusions:

1. ChatGPT can be another layer of defense you can use when self-editing. ChatGPT can help you create cleaner manuscripts before sending them to your editor.
2. When used with good self-editing and current tools like Word, Grammarly, ProWritingAid, and PerfectIt, ChatGPT can free up your editor to look for more significant problems in your story rather than focusing on routine spelling and grammar errors.

This sort of tool will never replace an editor because the value of an editor is far more than spelling and grammar errors. The most valuable skill that an editor brings to the table is catching things that no computer ever could, such as plot holes, inconsistencies (such as a character standing out twice), and other issues related to research, character development, and plot.

Isn't it amazing that we are moving toward a future where spelling and grammatical errors may well be things of the past? In the future, authors and editors will spend very little time fiddling with the mechanics of sentences and more time tweaking story elements. To me, that's a win for everyone. I imagine that the editors of the future will be using these tools too.

Anyway, I ran more tests on ChatGPT. Because I keep lots of data about my editing analytics, I also ran a test to see how "clean" my previous book manuscripts could have been if I had run them through ChatGPT. After all, if the tool had found more errors, I would have had cleaner manuscripts. I found that ChatGPT could have reduced my edits by *at least* 50 percent.

Again, there is never any substitute for an editor, and authors who use this technology to bypass editing altogether are foolish in doing so to their detriment. But this is yet another tool we can use to create cleaner manuscripts, satisfy readers, and become the writers of the future.

# STRATEGIC DEFENSE IN THE AGE OF AI

As I wrote in previous volumes of the series, 2022 was a watershed moment for AI art. It was also a watershed moment for AI in general.

Even if you don't use AI applications in your writing or the production of your books, you still have to contend with it. Even if you are stolidly against AI and everything it stands for, it still poses a substantial business risk, and not in the ways you might think.

As I have written ad nauseam, it is dangerous to use AI art right now. There is also some risk in using AI text generation tools such as Sudowrite. This is because these AI models were trained on copyrighted work that the developers did not have permission to use (potentially, if their use is not deemed fair use by a court). For this reason, the use of any AI tool could constitute unexpected copyright infringement, though I do think the chances of this are rare if you use some basic due diligence, such as not including artists in your prompts and scrutinizing your images for evidence of trademarks.

The real risk is this: even if you don't use AI in any capacity, there's no guarantee that someone you hire won't. For example, how will you know for sure if your cover designer isn't using MidJourney or Stable Diffusion? If they are, they could commit copyright infringement, and you will be the one who gets sued.

If you hire someone for copywriting or marketing services, it could well be using AI tools for the output. If you hire a programmer, they could also be using AI-generated code. There is risk no matter where you look, and you have to be more defensive than you were in the past.

One way to solve this problem is through a written contract. Two clauses in particular could help with setting expectations for freelancers. The first is a warranty clause that states that the designer warrants that their work will not be partially or fully rendered by AI. If it is, they should be required to provide any prompts and source material. The second clause is a hold harmless and indemnification clause, which indicates that the designer will hold harmless and indemnify the writer for any allegations of copyright infringement arising from the work.

I know, I know... Writers don't like to draft contracts with freelancers. It's not customary.

However, in this new future we're moving into, we simply don't have a choice.

This year, I was fortunate to be invited to the Superstars Writing Seminar run by Kevin J. Anderson in Colorado Springs, Colorado. I had heard great things about Superstars over the years, and this was my first conference.

Frankly, it was the best writing conference I have attended thus far in my career. This chapter will recap my experience there, advice I learned, and a few "level-ups" that netted me major wins during my time there.

**Visiting Superstars**

I had seven events to prepare for:

1. A book signing
2. A panel on estate planning
3. A panel on productivity
4. Part one of a talk on my book *Be a Writing Machine*
5. Part two of a talk on my book *Be a Writing Machine*
6. A VIP dinner with seven authors who paid to have dinner with me

7.  Career counseling sessions with those wanting
    specific advice from me
8.  A final Q&A panel with the instructors


Wow. It was an unbelievably jam-packed conference, and I was "on" from 7AM to midnight every night. I had no downtime.

Honestly, I like it that way. I'm such an introvert that I enjoy switching to an extrovert for a few days 1) because I know there will be a definite end to it and 2) I accomplish a lot of networking in such a short time.

There were approximately 300 people at the event. It was big enough that you couldn't meet every person there, but small enough that you could easily find whoever you were looking for if you wanted to.

The community at Superstars is unlike any I have attended. Every conference has its strengths and value propositions. For example, 20BooksVegas is gigantic—there are so many people and speakers that you couldn't possibly attend all the events. That's a strength because it gives you so much flexibility in choosing how to structure your time. Everyone gets something different out of the experience. Plus, it's in Las Vegas, which is easy (and cheap) to get to, and you can't beat the food. Inkers Con is a smaller, more intimate conference with more structure and support for its members. The conference does an amazing job of bringing in great speakers, recording them with professional audiovisual teams, and creating evergreen material out of its yearly conferences. And so on.

Superstars' strength is its community. Everywhere I went, longtime members went out of their way to talk to me and ask how I was enjoying the conference. And they were sincere about it. Everywhere you looked, people were hugging like they were long-time friends. The hotel bar was so full every night that people were standing shoulder-to-shoulder. It was a sight to see, especially when you consider that all of those people were probably introverts!

And this community was diverse—it wasn't just aspiring writers. There were extremely successful authors in the ranks too, sharing their knowledge. There was also a mixture of traditionally published, self-published, and hybrid authors too. In short, this was a tribe where anyone, no matter their status in the writing world, could come, be welcomed for who they are and where they are in their writing career, and be supported. That's a wonderful thing to see. I've been to writing conferences where there is a clear dividing line between aspiring and professional writers. The two groups don't always mix so freely.

When I attend events as a speaker, I like to network and connect with other speakers. It is a great opportunity for collaboration, but I also enjoy speaking with aspiring writers. I enjoy answering their questions and helping them through the problems they're dealing with. This was one of the few conferences where I felt like I had great networking opportunities with speakers who were much further along in their careers than me, *and* where I gave lots of advice to authors just starting on their paths. I like it when I'm not the most experienced person in the room, and I also like it when people want to know about the experience I have.

In any case, visiting Superstars was a lesson in what hospitality should be in the writing community. We spend so much time online that we often forget that in real life, people are just people. All that noise on social media and people yelling and screaming at each other over stupid stuff doesn't matter. I am positive that there were many people at Superstars who held the exact opposite political views as me, but none of that mattered.

Superstars is an incredible tribe, and I am honored to be part of it.

I also met a few people who always wanted to meet in person. I had breakfast with Todd McCaffrey, best-selling writer and a judge for The Writers of the Future contest. (Oh, and he is McCaffrey's son.) Todd grew up in the traditional side of the business, but has embraced self-publishing. It was amazing to hear his stories about his mother, his experiments in self-publishing, and his best craft tips.

I had lunch with Joanna Penn, and we chatted about artificial intelligence, the future of publishing, and so much more. I have been on her show "The Creative Penn" three times, and chatting with her was like chatting with an old friend. I also came away with so many ideas that I intend to implement in my publishing business in the coming months.

I also had dinner with Dean Wesley Smith and Allison Long Guerra of WMG Publishing. Dean has been a mentor for me, and his advice has helped my craft jump to the next level. He has impacted me and changed my writing career in more ways than I can count. He gave me a lot of professional advice and also helped me with some ideas I have for Kickstarter.

I also had dinner with Dave Chesson, the creator of Publisher Rocket and the writing app Atticus. Dave is an amazing entrepreneur. We chatted about software, APIs, and all sorts of things that had nothing to do with publishing, but will be transformative in the next few years. I've said a few times in the series that Dave has one of the sharpest minds in publishing; in a meeting with him, I am doubling down on that.

I also had working lunches with other professional writers, and I came away from each one with so many ideas and to-do items. I have never come away from a writing conference with so many action items.

## Some Lessons Learned

In a talk entitled "Microsoft Word for Editing," editor Mia Kleve covered the basics of using Microsoft Word. I like to think that I am an advanced Word user. I have taken countless courses and spent a lot of time learning the tool to be in the top one percent of users when it comes to productivity. However—and this is why I attended—I picked up a few tips from the talk that I either forgot about or didn't know. I also walked away from the talk with three book recommendations to deepen my understanding of Microsoft Word macros, wildcard searches, and how editors think about punctuation. In previous volumes of this series, I discussed how I am obsessed with learning how editors see the world. By learning how they think, I can learn how to create cleaner manuscripts quickly and efficiently. So, listening to a professional editor share how she uses Microsoft Word was immensely valuable.

In a talk entitled "Public Speaking for Authors," professional speaker Kate Dane shared her best tips for authors to get over their fear of public speaking and use their books as a platform for sharing their expertise. The talk was aimed at beginners who are terrified of speaking. Sure, while I have substantial public speaking experience, I can always learn more. The talk helped reinforce public speaking basics that I have always followed. Kate also shared an exercise that I found useful for helping people identify their strengths as a speaker.

In a talk titled "The Creator Economy," Joanna Penn discussed the transformative technologies that are coming to the self-publishing space. The things that Joanna is doing with Shopify are nothing short of amazing. She also discussed the Patreon model, which I currently use. She discussed author Seanan McGuire and how she uses Patreon to distribute short stories to her readers ahead of publication. That gave me an idea. Right now, I am submitting short stories to all the professional markets. At the time of this writing, I have a short story at every professional market that will take one. I've been wrestling with what to do with the stories when all the markets reject them. I will be starting a short story series where I self-publish all of the stories rejected by magazines, as well as accepted stories as reprints. The idea I got from the talk was to share stories with my patrons as soon as they are rejected from all magazines, but *before* they are published in the anthology series, which could take some time because I am putting five stories in each book (and those stories all have to be rejected first). This single tip will help me improve the value of my patronage on subscriptions.

On a panel titled "Should I Write Short Stories," panelists discussed the benefits of using short stories to further one's author career. The panelists were Todd McCaffrey, best-selling author and judge of the Writers of the Future contest; Jonathan Mayberry, best-selling author and one of the winningest authors in history when it comes to awards and prizes; and John Goodwin, president of Galaxy Press, the official publisher of L. Ron Hubbard and the Writers of the Future contest. The panel reinforced the reasons I write short stories:

- To practice my craft
- As a marketing tool
- To experiment with new genres, styles, and writing techniques
- To "test" new ideas and forays into new genres

I asked the panel for their best tip on getting out of the slush pile. John gave an amazing answer that made me realize I had been doing things wrong for the past six months. He said (paraphrased), "Submit to the Writers of the Future contest, do your best to place either as a winner or an honorable mention, and then include that accolade in your cover letter." According to him, it is a great way to rise out of the slush pile because magazines respect the contest and placing there (even if not a winner) is taken seriously. Considering that I placed twice as a Silver Honorable Mention, that was an instantly practical tip that I could start using immediately. I kicked myself for not having thought about that until John said it. You can bet I rectified my mistake immediately!

The panel also gave another tip that resonated with me. Jonathan Mayberry told a story that he had heard from someone that they had heard about Dean Koontz (super scientific, and like a game of telephone, I know, but we're talking about Dean Koontz here). To paraphrase the story, Dean Koontz had difficulty transitioning from novels to stories, so he developed a technique to help him make this transition easier and write stories quickly and effectively. The legend is this: he would write the first few pages of the story to get a feel for the world and characters. Then, he would jump ahead and write the ending. After that, he would write the rest. He felt this was a more economical and efficient method because it saved him from tangents that short stories often take one down.

Often, I know the ending of a short story as soon as I get into the world. Very few short stories have surprised me. I usually know where I'm headed after one or 2,000 words. This is not the case with novels. What if I tried it? What would I have to lose? According to Mayberry, the trick allowed him to write short stories much faster. It's worth considering.

In a talk titled "Estate Planning for Authors," attorney Paul Mason confirmed many of the things I wrote about in my book *The Author Estate Handbook,* but he went deeper on some concepts that I hadn't considered. In his opinion, power of attorney is the most important legal document when developing your estate plan. He acknowledged wills and living wills, but he brought some blind spots to the audience's attention. A power of attorney should be specific, and it should include a list of specific tasks that the appointee has the authority to do. Otherwise, institutions such as banks (or even book retailers) may not allow it. This is because attorneys are terrified of making mistakes when it comes to heirs and access. He highly recommended that power of attorney documents be updated with specific tasks.

He also explained the different types of powers of attorney.

- "Standing power of attorney" is power of attorney that you grant to be active at any time, not limited to a specific time or event.
- "Springing power of attorney" is power of attorney that you give to someone only upon your incapacitation.

There are also three ways the power of attorneys can end:

1. Death
2. Revocation by the person granting it
3. Expiration of a time limit

Part recommended to re-execute your power of attorney every few years because attorneys will hesitate to use very old ones for fear of it potentially having been revoked without their knowledge. He recommended doing this every three to five years and having your power of attorney notarized.

He also recommended looking into Q-TIP and marital trusts. He likened trusts to buckets that hold all of your things. In *The Author Estate Handbook,* I devoted a small chapter to trusts but explained that they were amazingly complicated and needed an attorney's expertise. This was a great session to ask questions about trusts.

Those were just a few of the many pieces of wisdom that I learned at the conference.

This section recaps the books I've published and media I've created during the quarter. To keep the book evergreen, I will not include links to podcasts or magazine articles because sometimes links break over time, especially with podcasts if the hosts stop podcasting. You can easily search for them to see if they're still active at the time you're reading this book. If they are, enjoy! If not, please accept my apologies.

## Magazine Articles

"Managing Chronic Illness as an Author (Interview with Roland Denzel)." *Indie Author Magazine*, February 2023.

# READ THE NEXT VOLUME

Michael's writer journey continues in the next volume of this series!

Grab your copy at www.authorlevelup.com/confidential.

# MEET M.L. RONN

Science fiction and fantasy on the wild side!

M.L. Ronn (Michael La Ronn) is the author of many science fiction and fantasy novels including *The Good Necromancer*, *Android X,* and *The Last Dragon Lord* series.

In 2012, a life-threatening illness made him realize that storytelling was his #1 passion. He's devoted his life to writing ever since, making up whatever story makes him fall out of his chair laughing the hardest. Every day.

*Learn more about Michael*<br>
www.authorlevelup.com (for writers)<br>
www.michaellaronn.com (fiction)